The Ghost Was
Always The Machine

The Ghost Was Always The Machine

Poems by RJ Walker

BLUE SKETCH PRESS | PITTSBURGH

The Ghost Was Always The Machine
Copyright © 2021 RJ Walker

This edition published in paperback by Blue Sketch Press
1 5TH Street, Sharpsburg, PA 15215
www.bluesketchpress.com
Executive Editor: Jesse Welch

Cover Image: Aimee Voss & RJ Walker
Interior & Cover Design: Little Owl Creative (littleowlcreative.com)

No part of this work may be reproduced, or stored in a retrieval system, or transmitted in any form or by any means, electronic, mechanical, photocopying, recording, or otherwise, without express written permission of the publisher or author, with the exception of educational institutions. Please write to Blue Sketch Press for information about permissions.

The Ghost Was Always The Machine
by RJ Walker—1st ed.

    ISBN (print)   978-1-942547-15-0 (trade paperback)
                            1-942547-15-0 (ISBN-10)

Cont**ents**

Entrance Exam

My Mother Explains My Depression to Me

Face Blind

Tin Man

Ice

The Fall

Afterglow Vista

Shapeshifter

The Shotgun

Shoelaces

Twilight

Ghost Story

Summer of Mania

Insomnia

The Little Engine That Couldn't and That's Okay

Ghost in the Graveyard

A Home

Arcades and Card Games

The News

The View

PTSD: An Escape Room

Polybius

About
Strategy Guide

The Ghost Was Always The Machine is an artist's book which blends **digital** and analog platforms. You'll be bouncing between this book and web pages. You'll only be able to access the web pages with passwords which can be deduced from the content of the poems and the hints laid out in the analog portion of the book.

The poems in this book must be exhumed, peeled apart, summoned, disassembled, and re-assembled. It is strongly encouraged that you take notes. Write in this book. Dog-ear the pages. Bookmark websites. Use the book as an umbrella. Eat pizza off of it. Make this book your own. There are more poems than are listed in the table of contents. You'll have to be clever if you want to find all the poems.

I'm not going to lie, this is a heavy book with heavy poems in it. I've had depression for a long time, and it made me a target for bullying and harassment throughout my youth and school life. I found relief in books, video games, comics, and anime. I grew up in a very religious Mormon family, and to them, the solution was simple. Add more Jesus. I graduated from seminary, was an eagle scout, and the final piece of the Mormon Tri-force was a Mormon mission. While I dedicated myself to Jesus, my depression only got worse. Surprise, but sending a mentally ill person to a 2-year religious excursion with extremely strict rules far away from anybody they know... isn't the cure for depression. It did, in fact, make my mentall illness much much worse.

I didn't sleep for 2 weeks and ended up having a seizure, hitting my head and causing a traumatic brain injury. The church sent me home, but to my parents, it was obvious what happend. I didn't have enough faith, and I had given in to the temptations of the devil. I was disowned, and I had become homeless. To survive, I sold my Pokemon cards, samurai swords, video games, and comics until I could get back on my feet.

It was a very slow process. I had lost my entire support network. I had no furniture or belongings but I did manage to find a job as an EMT and house myself. I couldn't afford to buy back my video game consloe, so I would go to a nearby arcade. It was dingy and rotting away but they had several rare cabinets and it was really all I had. Ever since, whenever I wanted to kill myself, I'd go to that arcade instead.

The arcade was a symbol of survival for me. It seemed like a place out of time. A sort of purgatory. Often, I found that I didn't want to die, I just wanted to leave the world. The old arcade allowed me to do that. The arcade never did well, financially. It was clearly a passion project for some eccentric collector of rare arcade machines. They technically closed at 3am, but nobody would ever come to lock the doors so it was always open for me. During the 2020 pandemic, it finally closed its doors for good.

```
This book is dedicated to

    the Atomic Arcade
   Emmigration Canyon
       My Bathtub
     My Sleeping Bag
      The Staircase
 Greenhouse Effect Coffee

And all the other places
           and
   people that didn't
       let me die.
```

Oh, and you'll need this later. Don't forget it. To decode use a QWERTY keyboard. Shift the letters to the left by one and you'll find the answer.

Entrance Exam

Before reading this book, you must first pass the entrance exam.

This is an open note test. Please sit down at a computer and make sure you are free of distractions. You may use a phone, but ensure that you are on the desktop version of the exam website.

The password is: **entranceexam**

https://www.decodethecity.com/blank-page

My Mother Explains My Depression to Me
(After Sabrina Benaim)

There was a great storm at sea
The disciples were afraid the ship would get swallowed up
now read
read
read what Jesus said
read it
he said
"Why are ye fearful, O ye of little faith?"
Then he arose, and rebuked the winds and the sea;
and there was a great calm.

See
she says
See
Don't you feel better?

    and she does not know
    that I tried to drown myself
    accidentally on purpose
    for the 2nd time today.
    but that is too much to say
    so I say
    No
    I am not Jesus
    and I have depression, not a storm

She says
We all know you just made this whole thing up
to get out of going on your mission
You don't have depression
you just don't have enough faith
Jesus said so

but it's ok

look, keep reading,
about the two men, possessed with devils
They say
> **"If thou cast us out, suffer us to go
> away into the herd of swine."**
And Jesus says "GO" and sends them into the swine

and they drowned
they drowned
that's why It's ok.
      She holds my head underwater and says
Because it wasn't you
you got a devil in you
so we get it out
and you can stop with that limping
and storming yourself to death
and go back on your mission
teach those folks in Texas
about the Jesus who saved you
from the devil in you.
We'll baptize it out of you
yeah, yeah
I know it. I know it to be true. I Prayed about it
it's the truth
the truth

The truth is a drowned pig
a ship at sea.

You are His tool, RJ
Jesus doesn't let his tools rust
not like your father
because we all know I didn't give this to you
this sad boy disease you made up
the devil you got in you
with his cigarettes
and corona
So I'm gonna divorce this devil out of you
yup yup it works
worked for me

    I say
I don't want to be Jesus' drowned pig
    I say
I want to die
    But I fail to want myself to death

    but she comes close when She says
You WILL go back on your mission
you WILL fulfill your purpose
Kill the parts of yourself that are yourself

    I say
    I'm trying
    she says

You,
You are the anti-christ
Jesus said so
Keep reading look
look, look what jesus said
he says
"Your son is a broken ship at sea
and he keeps trying to splinter himself
because he hates Me
he hates God

He hates You."

How could you do this to me?
After everything I've done
taught you how to be a blade
so stop goshdang cutting yourself

How dare you hurt me with your hurt
How dare you Kill Jesus with your killing.
He died your death to death and now you can't die
so you can't get away

> I say, in the voice of all my suicide attempts
> each one a pig,
> a shipwreck
> Drowned at sea

What have we to do with thee, oh son of god
art thou come hither to torment us before the time?

She hands me the whole violent ocean and says
Go then,
You vile thing,
I will not have you in this home that is your home
I will not have you die in this coffin that is your room
because it was never your room
all this
all this was mine,
it was mine and I gave it to you

wretched beast
I cannot bear the sight of you
my son who has eaten my son
and wears his bones
I take back my motherhood
and give you stones,
no go forth into the swines
and drown.
"GO"

She waits for me to respond.
But I have too much to say.
Yet I manage to say it all.
in a single word.

Goodbye.

Ghost in the Graveyard

We're playing night games.
Call to RSVP

(274) 721-0531

Face Blind

When I was 19
I didn't sleep for 2 weeks and had a seizure
and I fell down and hit my head

That's two decapitations
right in a row
and my head came clean off twice
and cracked like a frozen lake
and all my childhood memories
fell through the ice and drowned
in water so cold and deep
that it grabs you by the spine
and shakes the language off of you
like autumn leaves.

I have a memory disorder now
Prosopagnosia.
Facial blindness.
Faces don't get stored in my memory
so everyone is a stranger
and for a long time
I didn't know what deep dark lake
this loneliness crawled out of.

Sometimes I'll be writing in my notebook and look up
and see someone staring at me
like I was the one staring at them

and then they'll copy my movements
and then I realize that I am looking at a mirror
and the stranger is me.

This is the Alone disease.
It is impossible to recognize
the people who have loved me
or who I have loved.
I can only see someone
by looking at them
so when they are gone
they are gone gone.
and it is just me
who I also don't remember
or recognize
and the cracks grow wider
and they grow deeper
and they grow arms and legs and fingers and claws
and a hunger for something they cannot swallow.

I have learned to recognize people by their voices.

I can hear a laugh in a crowd
and know that you are there.

I can play a song in my head
and hear your voice singing it.

Remembering your face
is like catching the wind
yet I can hear your voice being carried by it.

and that hurts
far worse
than any flavor of forgetting.

Loss is just loneliness
with a masters degree.

This shattered ice memory is only skilled
in remembering all the ways
I have been hurt.

I am writing in my notebook
and I look up and someone is staring at me.
I think they know me.
it isn't a mirror this time.
I am afraid.
This person
could be anybody.
It could be you.
The wind blows.
I try to catch it
but I don't hear
a thing.

Tin Man

Oh, Great And Powerful Oz
Your tin man has come back
to return the heart he was given
I think it's broken

I wore it back to the woods
to cut down trees like I used to
But then the trees started screaming
and they wouldn't stop screaming
and it didn't used to hurt like this
Before it was just loud lumber
and not a thing that hurts you when it hurts

So, please, Take it back.
I'd rather rust in the woods
than hurt the woods again,
look at me,
I'm a metal man
my body is an axe blade now
cutting is all I have become
and if I cannot cut down trees
then the only thing I can cut down
is myself.

Did I ever tell you how I lost my first heart?
The witch cursed me
with a body that cannot live with itself
and one by one my axe removed pieces of me

Anxiety—it is my cutting disease
How else might I have a hand that cannot harm
or a chest that cannot hurt
than through the removal of all my pieces
I cut myself up
so the hurt has a smaller container
to fill

Depression
It is my rusting disease
The curse of heaviness
The curse of hollowness
It is not a desire to die
it is a desire to not live
The difference between a tree
and the axe rusting in its trunk
The difference between a man
and a hollow empty kettle

Oz, this heart
I feel the curse of the witch
split it open like a log.
Screaming and bloody
just like those damn trees in that forest
and I know I deserve it
for what I have done to them
I do not know which is worse
Being full of hurt
or being empty of everything
To be an axe
or to be a rusted lump

I beg of you
Please take this bleeding thing
I am too depressed to live
but too anxious not to

I can neither care for this heart
nor live without it
keep it safe
keep it far away
from me

Arcades and Card Games

You've
got
A
Tube sock
Full of
~~Quarters~~
Prayers

You need
to spend
them to

Survive.

https://www.decodethecity.com/blank-page-1
(Remember to use the desktop version of the site)

Ice

A man has frozen to death
in pioneer park
while the city council
argues
over which neighborhood
to put the new homeless shelter in.

Salt Lake City Winters
do not care
about property values.
About the cost of living.
About tourism money
Salt Lake City Winters
only care
about the greatest snow on earth.
A man in pioneer park
is buried under 6 feet
of the greatest snow on earth
and residents of the Sugar House neighborhood
All pitched in for his Headstone.
"Here Lies No Shelter on Simpson Ave
One out of 58 frozen to death this year
a new high score
since the recession"

My conservative family
says he deserved to die.

That their tax dollars
shouldn't pay for anyone else's survival.
That warmth is a privilege
not a right.

My liberal friends
say how hard they worked
to beautify this neighborhood
so it doesn't look like a "ghetto."
Say they should put the homeless shelter
somewhere nobody lives
the middle of the desert.
A corral for those they consider "undesirables,"
as in, a ghetto.

A man has frozen to death
in pioneer park
while my liberal friends
and conservative family
bicker about how to bury his body,
with dirt
or with gentrification.

And the new homeless shelter is canceled
because my liberal friends protested it
to save the crystal shop/vegan sandwich store.
Because my conservative family protested it
to reallocate their tax dollars to something important
like fighting the public health crisis of Pornography.

And my friends and family do not know
when I was homeless
and I slept in the canyon
and the ice was an undead thing
with their faces
and my tears were ice in my beard
and I had failed to kill myself again, that night
and the frost had come to finish the job.

The Fall

On my
on   my
on   my
mormon mission
I
        i   I

had a
    m
     a
    nic episode
and i
and   i didn't
sleep for
to too two weeks
and
   I
       had a
had a
    hada
h   ad a head.
hit my   SIEZURE.

It caus
ed

Permanent
    brain
brain damage

brain
                        damage.

It effected affected m y

Motor
    fu
          funct
fuf
skills.
And my
me-m
ory.

I aqu
aquired
got
ended up with
dy   s
| ex
ia.
and
n' na
a
facial blindness.

A De-pressiv-e e-p-i-s-o-d-e
a
s
    t
        u
           u
              s
                 t
                    u
                       s
                          t

u   tt

stutter
anna limp.

I hadta walkwitha stick
I would
\
  \
       fall.

I t took m o nths

        to
R   E   C   O   V   E   R.

My brain
started to repair what damage it could.
and oh how heavy \
heavy
     my   I C A R US
legs
     These burning W I N GS of iron and wood, stricken
from the sky
yet walking on water like   they shouldn't

Bless the healing ritual of cells.
     Bless the microscopic power of recovery
how something so small
     did more than their big God ever could.
More holy than jesus
     this flawed biology
crawling from the sea to the mud to the land
     growing legs like   it shouldn't.

Bless that wooden walking stick
     Bless the forest which grew the wood
bless the workers of the harvest
     bless the harvest
o mighty factory workers- bless you too
and your hourly wage glory
     hallowed be thy power
which held me up
when I wanted the staircase to kill me
but it wouldn't.
When god and all his angels

broke my back and my heart's back.

Hallelujah this world
hallelujah the
\
  \
    fall

Hallelujah this world
hallelujah the
\
  \
    fall
both a crash and a tumble into wonderland
hallelujah this earth
which loves you as much and as little as any god would
but the big difference between god and earth
is that when you fall
the earth
        will
al   ways

C   A   T   C   H YOU

Afterglow Vista

The mausoleum, in the woods
is a dinner table with 6 neatly
arranged chairs .
The chairs contain the ashes
of the dead
family.

The table rests
beneath the open sky
within a 7 pillar rotunda.
One of the pillars
is Broken / Intentionally.
Broken / by the father,
who designed this grave.

around the table
there is an empty   space

where a
chair ought to be.
This chair
belongs to the broken
pillar . it belongs
to me. because
it doesn't belong
anywhere.

when you leave
the family

religion, they
break / you
off of the family
tree, like a dead branch.

Tombs are **PLACES** for
good kids who
love the right
kind of jesus.
kids who don't
become absence.
They cease to be
kids and instead become
missing chairs
broken / pillars.

A child cAn become
unFinished to deaTh, you know.
LEt them disappoint long enough
and something must be undone
about them.
Isn't it so funny
how theiR Ghosts howL
when a family
weapOnizes death.

Those Who sit
in the chairs report an anxious discomfort
like they cannot be —
long. Like they neVer exISTed.
They say the chAirs are haunted,
the ghosts make any who dare
sit upon them
unwelcome. Afraid.
Every mother
and every father
ought to sit
in one of these haunted chairs
at least once.
This is what disownment feels like.
You don't belong
in this unfinished thing.

Leave
      get out
Leave
      get out
Leave
      get out
Leave

                                        The chairs may be
                              Haunted by some presence
                                  but the empty space
                                  you can stand there
                                      you'll feel just fine.

                                          there's nothing there.
                                there's nothing standing there

                                                      with you.

                                                      only me
                                          only this absence.

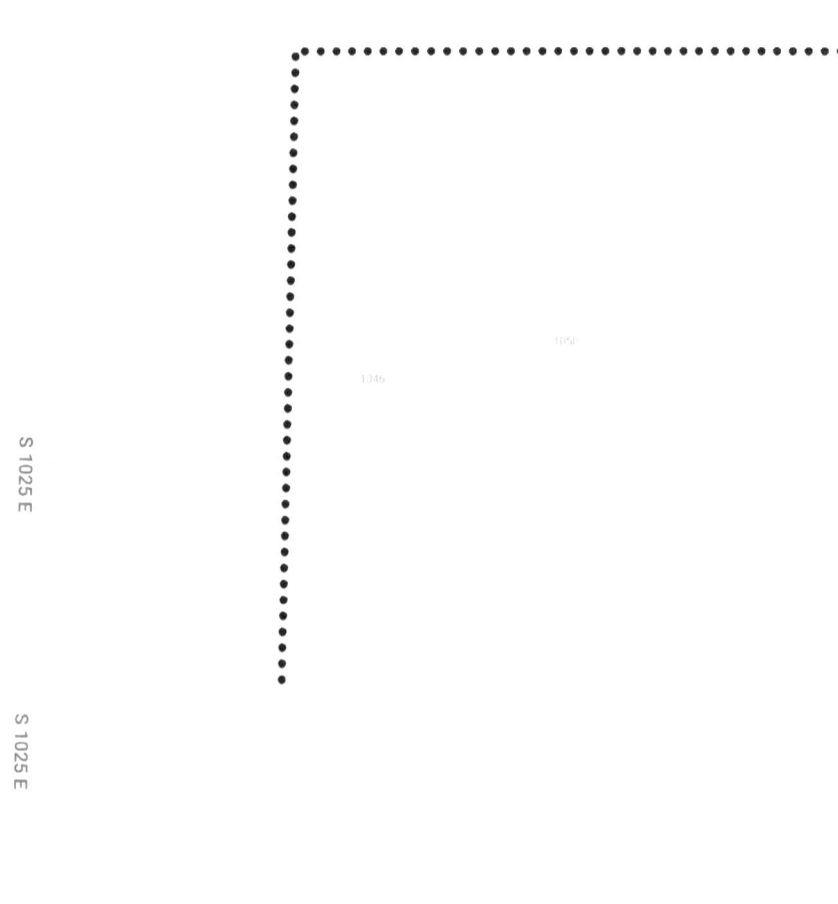

·······▶ A Home

A home is a place
      that you transform into
           The key to get inside is
                the house number

When the time comes,
Take your chance to **escape**

https://www.decodethecity.com/about-me-2

The Shapeshifter
After Salina Foster

I leave the ambulance with my partner
and begin approaching the crash,
the dead man in the desert
        And then I shapeshifted.
I became the burning engine
the death-rattle of a motorcycle
When a motorcycle dies, it becomes the road
and I am becoming the road
        And then I shapeshifted
I became the road
but I feel like one long headstone
bloody as a murder weapon
        And then I shapeshifted
I became the blood and bits of bone
the pieces of god's jigsaw puzzle
doomed to never again be a picture
        And then I shapeshifted
I became the empty boot fifty feet from its foot
it is a final emptiness
nobody would wear a dead man's boots
        And then I shapeshifted
I became the ambulance
bright lights and wailing like a dying beast
        And then I shapeshifted
I became the bits of brain matter
and i don't know anything
oh god i don't know anything

                    And then I shapeshifted
I became the nevada desert
and I will swallow all of this
I've swallowed a lot more, you know
                    And then I shapeshifted
I became a green medic responding to his first corpse
I feel like I'm getting paid to watch death do all the work
                    And then I shapeshifted

PTSD: AN ESCAPE ROOM

The View

Notes:

The first lock opens with a:

The second lock opens with a:

The combination for the third lock is:

If you want to see
The View
the password is
The first letter of each word

https://www.decodethecity.com/about-me-3

The Shotgun

Before I was born my great uncle shot himself in the head with a shotgun. A spray of lead angels and bloody devils blown right up into heaven. Dad always said that room in Grandma's house was haunted. But it was never the room that was haunted.

Look everyone   this is the shotgun I was born holding.
I brought it to show and tell.   I carry it in my spine now
sometimes in my forearms   or in my skull.

If you look down the barrel
you'll see my great uncle looking back at you like a periscope.
All Vietnam and wailing like his mother
so loud you'd think it was loaded.

Because it is.
When you aim down the sights,
you can hear him.
**"It doesn't matter what you're aiming at.
What matters is how you feel when you aim it."**

See the notches carved into the barrel?
Someone was punishing the shotgun in their arms
for not being wings.
            All those cuts have the same last name as me.

Bet you wanna know why the stock is shaped like a bottle.
Bet you wanna know why the hammer is shaped like a lover.
Bet you wanna know why the trigger   is shaped like nothing
   but a trigger.

Sometimes at Night,   I shiver so loud
all the shotgun shells fall out.
They all have my name on them.

Eviction Notice

Yesterday a dead
bird was
taped to my bedroom door.
I held it in
my hands.
my landlord called it
an eviction notice.
She wants to turn my room
into an Airbnb.

I did not call it
an eviction notice
I called it
a 9 year song
that never got an ending-
this chirping creature
choked up on its last notes

15 days to vacate.
No cause eviction.
Empty bank account
and twelve credit hours
plus the black box production I'm in
plus the kids with too many poems
and nobody to tell them to
all during finals week.
you know it's enough to make

a boy feel
like a dead bird
or an eviction notice
or a 9-year song that didn't get to choose how to say goodbye.

The almond tree in the yard
fell over in the last storm.
Perhaps this dead bird
lost its nest there.
Perhaps it didn't see the storm coming
and never learned
how to migrate right.

Perhaps its landlord
turned its nest
into an AirBirdnBird
and it couldn't come up with
first and last months rent and a thousand dollar deposit
for a new nest.
So it took out a loan
and died of interest rates.

Relatable, little tweet tweet.
Relatable.

But at least I got a flock.
At least I got a swarm of wings to catch me
when mine break

So thank you.
Thank you for the feathers
A whole pillows worth.
Enough to make a bed
somewhere.
Enough to give a bird
a soft place to land for a while.
Dead as it is

it will get better.
It is a thing with feathers
after all.

Shoelaces

I don't tell the retail worker
at the vans store
why I like to wear vans.
I don't tell him because
he doesn't ask
he just goes to the back
to see what they have in my size.

If he did ask
gravel would tumble from my mouth.
Blood would drip from my chin
and he would say
"Huh, so, nothing with shoelaces then."

I lied to my mother when I was 6.
I pretended I didn't know how to tie
my shoes.
I did know.
The loop goes around the bunny ears
and you pull it tight.

I don't tell my mom
that I know how to tie my shoes
because at school, I am the bunny.
Loop around my neck.

When my shoes became untied

I would leave them untied
dangling snakes around my ankles
ready to bite and send me to the floor.

I wouldn't tie them
because, the moment I would bend over
Cole would push me over.
A bunny caught in a snare.
So, I pretended not to know
how to tie my shoes,
that I might not fall into his trap.

I got my first pair of vans
when my mother realized
I was never going to tie my shoes.
That was perhaps the first time
she gave up on me.

The retail worker
at the vans store
sweeps up the gravel and blood
falling from my mouth
"you must be a skateboarder."
he says.

The Ne-

The ~~Noose~~

The ~~Nude~~

~~The Tho-~~
The ~~the~~ the the
the the the the
the

Twilight

I was 13 years old when Twilight came out.
A book about sparkling emo vampires.
I was sold right then
But when I saw the girl I liked reading it
    I went straight to the school library
      and checked it out

I did not know
that holding a vampire romance novel
was a sin
against manhood.

Masculinity
It is a weapon of a god
with a bloodthirsty following.

When an older boy saw me put the book in my gym locker
He grabbed me by the throat
then reached down my pants and said
"just checking to see if you're still a boy"
And he wouldn't let go
until I spit
on the vampire book I just checked out.

And nobody would believe
that straight boys
would sexually assault

other straight boys
like it's practice.

How quickly do boys hands
become claws
when reaching for a body.

"This is just how boys are"
                My mother tells me
                like it is only a moonless night
"Be a Man"
my father demands.
with blood on his teeth

"Son, In this world
there are predators
and prey."

as if I had to pick one.

And I knew then that my father
likely sank his fangs into
a version of me in a 1970's locker room.

Abuse is a curse you can pass through blood.
How a vampire makes a victim into another vampire.

Getting slapped in the genitals
is called "squirrel tapping"
and not sexual assault.

Smearing your crotch sweat
on another boy's face
is called "duck wiping"
and not sexual assault

And what a funny joke it is
to play with your food.

Drain it of its life
until it becomes what you are.

And the horror is not just the abuse
The horror is knowing
What I could have become.

    Donald Trump says through his fangs
    "It's just locker room talk"
    And in a locker room somewhere
    there is a younger version of me
    with another boy's sweat smeared on his face
    Exsanguinated.
    The president's words echo off the tile
    and a 13-year-old frame
    grows fangs.

The ~~the the quick~~
quick brown f- f-
~~fuck.~~ the the

Ghost Story

On a night just like tonight
There was a kid just like you-

>See, all good ghost stories
>happen on nights just like tonight
>And there's gotta be a camp fire
>it's not a proper ghost story
>without a campfire,
>Here, you, you be the campfire
>inviting and harsh and hungry
>just like that.
>
>and ghost stories are always
>happening to you
>or someone just like you
>so it might as well be you.
>And there's always a quivering silence.
>No ghost story is a story without
>a quivering silence.
>You, you be the quivering silence.
>Like a taut wire
>like you're about to break someone's heart,
>But don't quite know the best way
>to say the disaster you intend to.
>just like that.

On a night just like tonight

there was a kid just like you
And what a fool they were—

> See, ghost stories
> they only happen to fools
> because fools deserve to be haunted
> that's the moral of every ghost story
> They always make some critical mistake-
> wandering off alone,
> sneaking out without telling anyone,
> something like that.
> And you, you can be the mistake
> One that scares the libido right out of a teenage body
> One with a smile
> that doesn't know how sharp its teeth are.
> Just Like That

On a night just like tonight
there was a kid just like you
and what a fool they were
mixing love and depression like that.

> Ok so,
> you be the love, and all its obsession
> and you, over there,
> you be the depression and all Its obsession.
> The people sitting between you, you all
> are going to be the fine line
> between love and depression
> We'll call you regret
> and you are a terrifying
> human-centipede monster
> writhing and awful and everyone is the ass.

On a night just like tonight
there was a kid just like you
and what a fool they were

mixing love and depression like that.
It's enough to make a butcher knife
take bites out of anybody.

>**Ok, so the butcher knife is the monster**
>**You, with the hair, you're the butcher knife**
>**and you're so fucking hungry**
>**And you, with the other hair, you're my hand,**
>**holding the butcher knife**
>**And you, you're my bleeding**
>**forearm and you cannot escape**
>**you are a trapped rabbit,**
>**Ain't it scary that your closest friend**
>**has allied itself with the monster**
>**what a twist.**

On a night just like tonight
there was a kid just like you
and what a fool they were
mixing love and depression like that
it's enough to make a butcher knife
take bites out of anybody.
And it hurts, but it doesn't hurt
and that just isn't good enough.
So they went into the bathroom
turned the lights out
and said
"make it stop" 3 times
into the bathroom mirror.

>**Ok, so you, you're the ghost,**
>**you are my bathroom mirror**
>**You have teeth of glass**
>**and you're even hungrier than**
>**butcher knife was**
>**and you smile like a cliffside**
>**You open your mouth wide**
>**to reveal my many pills that have built**

half finished cities on your shelves.
And you, in the shirt, you are the pills
and you, next to them,
you're the vomit beast they make out of me
And you, in that empty chair,
you are the laughing nothingness.

so where were we,
the night
the kid
the depression and the knife

They turned the lights out
and said
"make it stop" 3 times
into the bathroom mirror.
And they try to overdose
but don't
because they can't do anything right
that is their curse.
And they are still haunted to this day
and every night is just like that night
hemorrhaging ghosts from the bathroom
And it can happen again,
especially on nights just like tonight.
    The scariest ghost stories
    have endings
    that aren't over yet.
    and me, I get to be that ending.

```
quick    brown    f-x
jumped   over-    the
the   lazy  f-x,   no
the     quick    brown
fo-  the  quick
```

quick brown f-x
jumped over- the
the lazy f-x, no
the quick brown
f0- the quick qui
quack br the

ju   mp
 ed

o
v
ju ju ju

jumpped ov   er

t-h-e
  la

j-o-t lz

d..dddddddddddd

The ~~No~~ News

~~The~~ The quick brown ~~facts~~ fox jumped over ~~the the the the the the the the the the the~~ the lazy ~~dog~~ dad

More on this breaking story as it unfolds.

The password is the subersive carnivore involved in this tragic story.

https://www.decodethecity.com/about-me-4

Summer of Mania

Alright, opening scene
It's the first day of Summer
I walk into frame
holding a 6 pack of Rockstar Recovery
energy drinks.
I almost died on tour in the spring
and I am desperate to know
what recovery tastes like.
So I drink all 6
and feel a neckbeard Jesus
piston kick my limbs into gear

Cut to
Explosive diarrhea from too much caffeine.
This is not what healing is supposed to feel like.
It's disgusting and messy
and neckbeard Jesus is
laughing in the stall next to me

Cut to
the last day of summer
I don't know why I'm yelling
but I do know that something has hurt me
and that thing was probably me

Cut to
Why am I so bad at sleeping and so good at hurting

Cut to
It's July, I'm a tree
sprouting from the stump
of another tree
dreaming of bird nests
and old forest fires
cut
cut
cut
cut

Cut to
This fucking mania
like an electric sun
automating these bad decisions
and making my mistakes so
efficient

Cut to
Credit Card Debt
from amazon shopping sprees

Cut to
What the fuck am I saying? Are these even words?
I need to shut the fuck up

Cut to
Dude, RJ, shut the fuck up.

Cut to
The first day of summer
5 out of 6 rockstar recovery drinks down
I don't think I can finish the 6th one
but goddammit
People only like Manic RJ

Cut to
Halfway through the summer
Everybody hates manic RJ
including Manic RJ?

Cut to
myself, my fuck up flesh
mania is a vibrating scizors
Summer is the only time that exists
so why even think of anything past it?

Cut to
I don't know.
Sometimes I am doing so much
I forget where I am
What day it is.
I fixate on whatever is right in front of me
to keep me from dissociating to death.
My friends think I hate them, because
all I can look at is my fucking hands.   Cut to

Closing scene
It's the first day of summer
It's June and I'm about to make
a terrible mistake
again and again and again.
I make my first cut and don't know
I will make so many more
Look at this poem
like last summer
all cut to pieces
in an effort to survive
the coming winter.
I bet if you unfolded it

It would look like a snowflake.

Hey, kid. Hey. There's a new game in the arcade. Don't play it. Don't. Don't. Don't. Don't. Don't. Don't. Play it. Don't play. It don't. play it play it play it play it play it

In the dystopian future of 1981 ███████████████ put a ██████████ arcade cabinet here as part of the ██████ ████████ mind control experiments. Everyone who has ████████████ this game has committed ██████████████.

The game was called ██████████████.

Insomnia

Every night

                        I wish could

go camping
Inside my own palms

                        Crack the moon
                        and   make   blankets

from its glowing guts.

I tried this once.
I nearly drowned.

So now,
I put my hands
over my eyes
And try to push the darkness
into them.

I do this for hours.

                        It doesn't work.

Help, I'm
[Redacted]
and there's
[Redacted]
and now I can't
[Redacted]
Because
[Redacted]

The Little Engine That Couldn't and That's OK.

Foreword:

So the other morning
I was too depressed to get out of bed
But also too anxious to stay in bed,

So I sort of slug crawled across the floor naked
With no clear direction.
It was during this tempest tossed moment
This "Lost at Sea" episode of despair,
That I decided to write this children's book.

Dedication:

For my mother
When I wanted to die the most
You called me the anti christ
And forced me out of the house.

**And now, for children's story time happy fun hour
I give you:
The Little Engine that Couldn't
And That's OK.**

Once upon a time
There was a train.
A train delivering nothing
To the city of nowhere.

For misguided reasons.

On the route
There was a very large hill.
Actually
It was a mountain
Actually it was it's own goddamn planet
But it looked like a hill.

And the train tried to go over this small hill.
And did not succeed.
"Come On" they all said
"You can do it!
You Just have to say
I Think I Can! I Think I can
You just have to try again and again"

And so the train tried again

"I think I can"
Thought the train.
Then the train became an eagle with no wings.
The eagle became a shipwreck
And the shipwreck became a boy
Who was so sad he had to walk with a cane
And the boy became the cane
His anchor to the floor
And the cane became collapsing
The collapsing became a heap on the floor
A pile a hurt
That could not stop shaking.
A diagnosis for psychosomatic limp.
When the depression is so bad
That a body
Cannot move
When the anxiety is so bad
That the body won't stay still.
Resulting in a limp

A collapsing
When all movement becomes de-railed
Like this story.

About How a person could be encouraged
To hurt themselves
      "I Think I Can"
But he couldn't.
He Stopped his car before it went off the cliff.
Put the pills away.
Left the knife in the drawer.
He couldn't do it.

      He tried again
And He couldn't do it.
He couldn't do it
He couldn't do it.

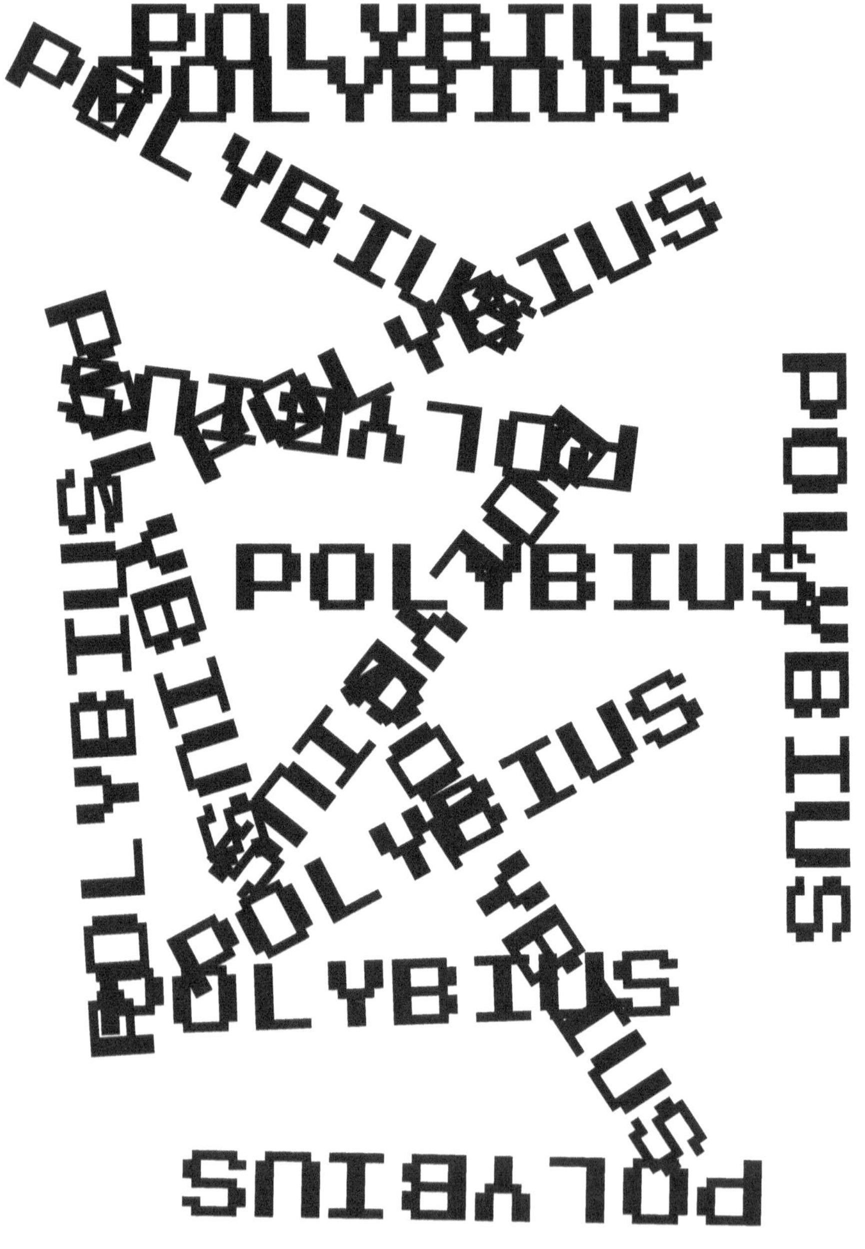
POLYBIUS
POLYBIUS
POLYBIUS
POLYBIUS
POLYBIUS
POLYBIUS
POLYBIUS
POLYBIUS

So, you made it
this far
very well.
You'll need this prayer

To access the arcade again, you'll need a password. It's a spell, or a curse. It's the hardest thing to say but the easiest thing to become. It's both loss and power. You'll need to decode it.

hpp fnur

https://www.decodethecity.com/about-me-5

Acknowledgments

"The Shapeshifter" previously appeared
in *Folio* literary journal

"Ghost in the Graveyard" previously appeared
in *Drunk in a Midnight Choir* online literary journal

About the Author

RJ Walker is a performance poet and voice actor from Salt Lake City, Utah. RJ has performed at the national poetry slam numerous times, representing Salt Lake City, and Sugar House Utah. At the Individual World Poetry Slam he was a showcased poet on final stage and placed 6th overall at the 2017 Individual World Poetry Slam. RJ won the NPS Spirit of the Slam award for organizing the first Compliment Deathmatch event. The next year he placed 4th at the National Poetry Slam with the Salt City Unified team. RJ Won the 2020 Button Poetry Video Contest with his poem "Face Blind."

He is the host and operator of The Greenhouse Effect Open Mic, SLC's longest running and most popular open mic style event. His poem, "Deceit & I," received viral reception on youtube and imgur, published in journals like A Plus, EMS1, and EMSWorld with over 500,000 cumulative Views.

www.ingramcontent.com/pod-product-compliance
Lightning Source LLC
Chambersburg PA
CBHW030350100526
44592CB00010B/900